Star Hawks

by Gil Kane and Ron Goulart

A Tempo Star Book

Distributed by Ace Books
Grosset & Dunlap, Inc., Publishers
New York, N.Y. 10010
A Filmways Company

Star Hawks
Copyright © 1977, 1978, 1979 by United Feature Syndicate, Inc.
All Rights Reserved
ISBN: 0-441-78150-0
A Tempo Books Original
Tempo Books is registered in the U.S. Patent Office
Published simultaneously in Canada
Printed in the United States of America

THE Star Hawks TEAM

GIL KANE is the chief cover artist for Marvel Comics. He is a three time winner of the coveted National Cartoonist Society award for "Best Comic Book Cartoonist." During his more than 30 years as a professional comic artist, Kane has drawn virtually every major adventure strip character from Batman to Flash Gordon. Kane was the artist instrumental in the development of Marvel Comics and has worked on just about every book in the Marvel line.

RON GOULART is one of science fiction's most prolific writers. He has had 200 stories and articles published in magazines ranging from *Playboy* to *Ellery Queen*. Goulart wrote his first novel, "The Sword Swallower," in 1968. Since then, he has written about 100 more under his own name and several pen names. His most recent works are, "After Things Fell Apart" (Ace) and "The Eye of the Vulture" (Pyramid).

WE DIDN'T MISS HER BY MUCH.

BUT WE MISSED HER... AND THERE'S NOT MUCH TIME!

SHE MUST HAVE SENSED WE WERE CLOSING IN, ILKA.

SHE'S GONE FROM THAT HOVEL.

YES, I HAVE CONFIDENCE IN YOU, RAKER...I KNOW YOU'LL FIND HER AND KILL HER!

DON'T WORRY... I'LL PICK UP HER TRAIL AGAIN.

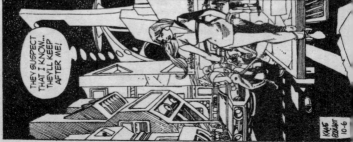

THEY SUSPECT THAT I KNOW... THEY'LL KEEP AFTER ME!

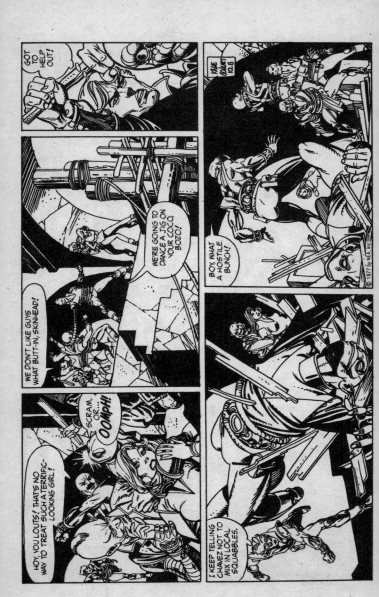

REX... A CRAMP! CAN'T SWIM....

DON'T SINK FOR A MINUTE....

...WHILE STAR HAWK CHAVEZ FALLS INTO THE OCEAN.

LITTLE BALDHEAD SIMP!

THAT'S ONLY ONE MAN'S... OOPS!

REX!

ON THE PLANET ESMERALDA, THE GIRL RUNS...

NO TIME TO STOP... MUST GET AWAY!

LOOKS LIKE YOUR SKINHEAD PAL'S GOING TO DROWN!

WHA-!

x

© 1977 by NEA, Inc.

WHY'S SHE SO ANXIOUS TO CONTACT EMPEROR RIAN?

PROBABLY TO WARN HIM...

TROUBLE IS... WE DON'T KNOW WHAT ABOUT!

DON'T WORRY, NAYDA!

I'LL SEE YOU GET EXACTLY WHERE YOU WANT TO GO!

TOO BAD NAYDA HAS EXTRASENSORY POWERS...

IT'S UNSETTLING TO MEET A SPLENDID-LOOKING GIRL WHO CAN READ MY THOUGHTS, REX.

MOST ANY GIRL CAN READ YOUR THOUGHTS, CHAVEZ, IT DOESN'T TAKE ESP!

EMPEROR NOT HERE...HUNTING TRIP IN NIGHTWOOD FOREST...EMPEROR NOT HERE...

NOT MUCH TIME!

GOT TO REACH THE NIGHTWOOD FOREST AND WARN HIM!

BUT HE ONLY USED A STUNGUN ON ME.

SO DID I FOR AWHILE THERE, REX....

I THOUGHT YOU WERE DEAD, CHAVEZ.

...THEN

SUPPOSE YOU TELL US WHAT'S GOING ON, NAYDA, AND WHY YOUR FAMILY SECURITY CHIEF TRIED TO KILL YOU...

WELL... I... I HAVE EXTRASENSORY ABILITIES...

I SENSE I CAN TRUST YOU... SO I'LL TELL YOU EVERYTHING.

MOST ALL WOMEN TRUST ME.

NOW I I KNOW WHERE AND WHEN!

THEY'RE GOING TO ASSASSINATE THE EMPEROR! THAT'S WHAT I FORESAW...

YOU RAN AWAY BECAUSE OF SOME KIND OF VISION YOU HAD?

YES, MY FATHER WAS DEAD... I DIDN'T KNOW WHOM TO CONFIDE IN. SO I RAN.

BUT THEN I REALIZED I HAD TO STOP THEM!

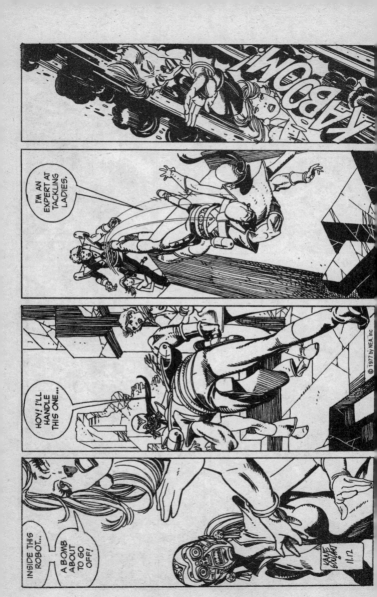

BEFORE LEO VERMILLION CAN FIRE HIS BLASTER... HE IS SHOT DOWN WITH THE DUSTER GUNS....

© 1977 by NEA, Inc.

THE TINKERS DID A VERY EFFICIENT JOB OF FOULING US UP, CHAVEZ!

KANE MOJAVE 1-3

SCAT! DÉPART!

GO ON YOU GUYS! LEAVE OUR SKYCAR BE!

NOW YOU...WON'T BE ABLE TO GO TRAIPSING OFF AFTER THESE TWO DESPERADOES!

THERE'S A BRIGHT SIDE TO THIS, CHUMS....

HOY, REX, THEY EVEN DISMANTLED MY LUNCHBOX.

...BEFORE THE REGIME'S TROOPS SWEPT THROUGH!

THIS WAS ONCE RICH, VITAL FARM-LAND, REX...

© 1978 by NEA, Inc.

FLYING LOW TO AVOID DETECTION, THE REBEL GIRL'S SKYCAR ARRIVES IN HER HOMELAND...

"HE'D BEEN A MILITARY MAN BUT THERE WAS NO PLACE FOR HIM IN THE NEW REGIME... FOR DIFFERENT REASONS WE WERE BOTH OUTCASTS NOW."

"THE TROOPS CAME FOR ME, TOO, TORBIN, A CLOSE FRIEND OF MY FATHER, DECIDED TO LOOK AFTER ME."

YOU HAVEN'T TOLD ME HOW LONG YOU'VE BEEN FIGHTING AGAINST THEM, ZERA.

NEARLY SIX YEARS...

...EVER SINCE MY PARENTS WERE TAKEN TO THE PRISON FARM TO DIE!

1-9

A SHOCKWHIP COILS ABOUT TORBIN'S NECK.

TOPPLING LIKE A GIANT TOWER, TORBIN CRASHES TO THE CAVERN FLOOR UNCONSCIOUS...

TOO MANY REGIME TROOPERS, TOO MANY SHOCKWHIPS EVEN FOR THE POWERFUL TORBIN...

THEY'RE NOT USED TO LIGHT!

THEY USUALLY SHUN IT!

LET'S HOPE THIS LIGHT HOLDS OUT UNTIL WE GET CLEAR OF THESE CAVERNS

© 1978 by NEA, INC.

GLAD YOU CAME TO WHEN YOU DID... YOU OKAY?

YES, YOU NEEDN'T WORRY ABOUT ME

KANE GOULART 1-25

ZERA GRABS REX'S LIGHTGUN AND SHINES IT ON THE DARK-LOVING NIGHTMEN...

...WHEN I FOUND MY PARTICULAR GENIUS COULDN'T *FLOURISH* UNDER GENERAL ZAKAR, I JOINED THE *REBELS!*

THOUGH I'VE BEEN DUBBED A *CONMAN,* I AM ACTUALLY A BUSINESS *GENIUS*...

SINCE YOUR OLD CAMP IS NO LONGER SAFE, WE'VE MOVED TO THIS ONE.

YOU'LL FIND THE ACCOMMODATIONS *FIRST RATE!* I DESIGNED THEM MYSELF!

WITH THE AID OF MY *AMAZING* SPY NETWORK I LEARNED YOU WERE HEADING FOR AN AMBUSH. I RUSHED TO THE RESCUE AND *DEFTLY* SNATCHED YOU FROM THE JAWS OF *DEATH!*

KANE GOLANT
1-31

ZERA, HOW DOES SHATTERBOX FIT INTO...

I DON'T THINK MY AFFAIRS ARE ANY OF YOUR...

IF YOU TWO TURTLE DOVES WILL CEASE SQUABBLING, I'LL EXPLAIN EVERYTHING *SWIFTLY* AND *CONCISELY!*

NOW TO MEET TAMMY!

AND IN THE ORBITING HOOSGOW...

NO DOUBT ABOUT IT. THIS UNDER-COVER WORK DETRACTS FROM MY OVERALL CHARM.

OH, I'M AWARE OF THAT, MR. CHAVEZ...

..."THIS IS MY WAY OF REMINDING YOU THAT YOU'RE NEVER TO TOUCH MY BODY!"

© 1978 by NEA, INC.

HOY, IT'S ME! CLEVERLY DISGUISED!

ZAM!

KANE KOUNT 2-12

AT THE REBEL CAMP THE RESCUE OF THE GIANT TORBIN IS BEING WORKED OUT...

BEFORE I BECAME A REBEL, I PLANNED SOME OF THE MOST AUDACIOUS CONS AND SCHEMES ON THIS PLANET...

...AND THIS TIME AROUND I'LL HAVE YOUNG REX CONTRIBUTING A HELPFUL NOTION OR TWO!

OH? IF IT HADN'T BEEN FOR HIM, TORBIN WOULDN'T HAVE BEEN CAPTURED AT ALL!

ABOUT READY TO EMBARK, TAMMY?

I CAN'T EXPRESS TO YOU HOW MUCH I'VE YEARNED FOR THIS MOMENT...

...FATHER!

AND AS USUAL YOU'VE NOTHING BUT SILENCE FOR YOUR ONLY SON!

© 1978 by NEA, Inc.

KANE GAULART 2-14

AT THE PRISON FARM...

PUTTING TORBIN IN CHAINS ISN'T A SMART MOVE.

I AGREE, BUT I'M NOT ABOUT TO TELL ZAKAR!

HE'S STILL POPULAR WITH A LOT OF PEOPLE!

VERY IMPRESSIVE, ZAKAR, AND VERY *WRONG!*

THANK YOU FOR THE COMPLIMENT, FATHER.

INSTEAD WE'LL BE USING IT FOR YOUR EXECUTION!

YOU PROBABLY INTENDED TO USE IT AGAINST ME...

© 1978 by NEA, Inc.

KANG BUART 2-17

NOW HERE'S AN INTERESTING WEAPON...

...THE DUSTER GUN YOU'VE BEEN SEEKING!

IN THE CONTROL CENTER OF THE PRISON FARM...

LEAVE ME NOW, CAPT. HODS!

I WANT TO SAVOR THIS EXECUTION IN SOLITUDE!

POWER STATION

...I CAN BRING OFF WHAT I PROMISED!

IF...

YOU'RE GOING TO SAVOR A FEW SURPRISES TODAY, ZAKAR!

KANG GUUM

2-1

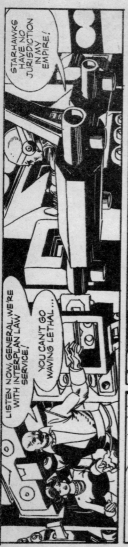

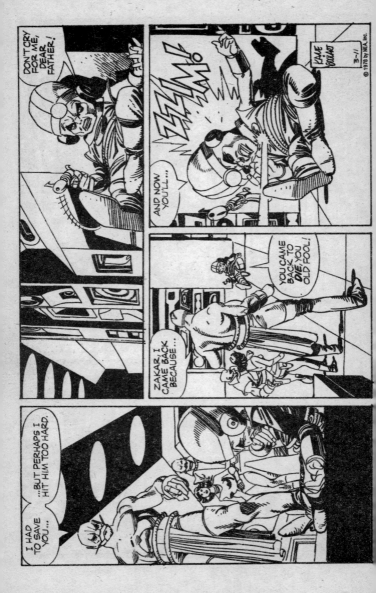

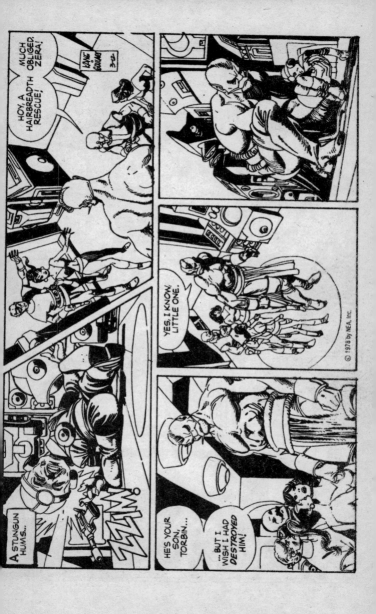